Brexit: W

Even with the big battalions lined up against Leave, the polls just wouldn't quit showing that Leave had a chance.. And then came Jo Cox, and it was all over.

You couldn't fight a victim whose birthday was on polling day. They kept the stories going all the time. We never had a chance, but turned up to vote anyway. And then history happened.

Here I try to capture the essence of what it was like for an old white non-thicko (Mensa, sorry), to vote Leave believing it was one of the most important opportunities in his life, and the extraordinary moments as the results came in.

It isn't over yet. Remain are determined to run roughshod over democracy to get their way after the 'wrong' result.

Here's what it felt like for one Leaver, and what he believes.

Andrew Mather

Brexit: Why We Won

#1 Best Seller Kindle Book on Brexit

#2 Best Seller Book on Brexit (based on e-Book alone)

Based on search 'Brexit' in Kindle Books and Books on Amazon.co.uk, as of 11th August 2016.

Other Books by Andrew Mather

ESSENE CAMELOT NOVELS

Apostle of Camelot

Warrior of Camelot

ROAD SAFETY SERIES

Experience Counts

One Source

BREXIT SERIES

Why We Won

Victory and Hope

A Sound Decision

Brexit: Why We Won

What Remain will Never Understand

About the Leave Victory

Andrew Mather

Revised August 2016

ISBN: 978-1537028149

Revised Edition

The original was written in a couple of days, and it showed, as some of the critics in the reviews legitimately pointed out.

With Remain up in arms against the result, it seemed appropriate to get something out that said that we'd achieved a great result for good reasons.

We've tidied it up, added a little organisation, and eliminated (mostly) the term luvvies, referring instead to 'liberals' or just Remain or Remainers.

It still won't be acceptable or palatable to Remainers, but as far as the vote is concerned, we did a sound and appropriate thing.

As time passes, news from Europe and the UK shows just how sound it was. We're doing nicely and self-interest and common sense are finally kicking in.

Things are looking good.

Andrew Mather

Introduction

On June 23rd the British People, comprising England, Wales, Northern Ireland, Scotland, Gibraltar and London, went to the ballot box to vote on a question: Should we Leave or Remain in the EU.

Even on the night I separated London out. It is an entity of 8 million people in its own right. More importantly it is where the liberals, the intelligentsia, the politicians and the money lives in a different world.

As I'm sure everyone knows, Leave won, by an overall margin of 52%:48% with a turnout of 72%.

It was a clear victory, regardless of what Remain have since tried to claim to invalidate the vote, of which more anon.

As I write this, in early July 2016, it is not clear that our politicians, solidly in the Remainer camp, will either implement the vote by invoking Article 50 and then negotiate a sensible settlement on our behalf, or whether they will find some excuse to ignore the vote, even re-run it as governments in Europe have done until they get the 'right' result.

As of August 21st, it seems that astonishingly, May is going to respect the vote. Given the uproar from

Remain, and their continuing manoeuvring, that was by no means certain. We'll see.

So the Resistance won, the Collaborators form the new government, and yet they're now being apparently loyal to a new independent Britain.

Our dependency on politicians to oversee the outcome from the vote has been one of the more disturbing aspects of the aftermath of the vote, once it became clear just how strongly the establishment was determined to Remain.

Ultimately, this was indeed a victory of the people over the politicians, foreign and domestic, the liberals, world institutions and and business interests including major US corporations.

I was less than impressed with the latter, seeking to interfere in the politics of a foreign nation, but from the home of the CIA, why should we be surprised?

As to our victory, Remain, derogatory as ever, have characterised that as being 'old white thickos' making the wrong decision.

Well, I'm two of those, but as a member of Mensa, not sure I can fairly be characterised as a thicko, and as to wrong, given the news in the media in Europe, and the absence of the sky falling on our heads, it seems more sound every day.

I believe that Leave voters made a very sensible decision, even if it may take years for Remainers to appreciate that. Some, however, it seems are already changing their tune. Dire prognostications of economic disaster are being turned into grudging admissions that we could do very well out of the EU.

Let me then try to describe to you why Leave won, as I see it. It may be of interest to Leave supporters who feel they did the right thing, but are disturbed by all the anger and hate directed at them. Those anger and hate are remarkably ignored by the mainstream media, while any hint of racism will get their full attention and be attributed to the Leave victory and voters.

In such an environment, when the same forces that were determined to Remain continue to resent the 'folly' of our vote, it should be understood then that what you have read has largely been driven by people with an agenda.

Amidst the 'doom and gloom' prognostications, the FTSE 100 within one week regained and surpassed the level of June 23rd, when Remain were a shoe-in. The next day it rose to the highest level since Aug 2015. Countries are lining up to sign trade agreements with the UK. The EU are acknowledging that there should be no red lines on immigration and control of our borders.

Across Europe there are 34 demands for referenda for other nations against the EU political system. The first optimistic posts are appearing about our future.

That has to be the fastest recovery in history from a 'catastrophe'. Perhaps it reflects the markets' confidence that Brexit will be overruled, or that we will go cap in hand to the EU to beg to have access to the free market, as indeed our politicians are doing. Perhaps it is genuine confidence as the new articles suggest.

We won't know for real whether the markets are rediscovering their confidence in Britain until after Article 50 has been invoked, and after we have left.

Nevertheless for now, let us take the opportunity to understand what happened, and why.

Reflections

I have no intention of offering a blow-by-blow account of the history and campaign. Many relevant items may be omitted, but in a sense they are by definition less relevant or irrelevant to me, and perhaps to many Leave voters.

This is rather a reflection of certain core issues and factors that led to our unexpected victory, a victory unexpected by Boris Johnson, by Nigel Farage, and by many if not all Leave voters, myself included.

Remainers will deride any sign that I am a 'little Englander', harking back to history, but the US repeatedly harks back to its Founding Fathers and its principles, and to a Briton, Agincourt, Camelot, and the like are no less elements that continue to fascinate, inspire and inform us.

Indeed, in order to counter the threats and claims of the Remainers, it has been apposite to remind them of our history vis a vis the French and the Germans.

Freeing Europe against political dictators has been a fairly constant occupation for this nation.

Likewise in the campaign running up to the vote, so was clarifying for Remainers that the EU is not Europe, it is a political system set above Europe. It seems that European leaders are particularly assiduous at deliberately conflating the two, speaking always of 'Europe' when referring to matters that are more properly issues about the EU political system.

Given the bitterness of the campaign and the aftermath, we may perhaps be forgiven for indulging ourselves in a whimsical comparison with equally unexpected victories in our history. There are indeed fitting parallels: the underdog, outmatched but it turns out not outfought.

Britons, the people of Britain brought up to tales of World War II, World War I, Napoleon, Elizabeth I, Agincourt, King Arthur, the Romans, are a bloody-minded race, not substantially different I would suggest from any other, but in this instance the bloody-mindedness served them well.

This was at its heart a people saying no to unelected autocrats, no to being told what to do, no to being told we couldn't decide our own future. Remain characterise it as a victory of racism over immigration, and we will look at those issues, but really it was fought and won for the same reasons we fought and won in two world wars: we don't like other people telling us what to do or threatening our freedom.

Remain's Reaction

I didn't give much thought to Remain's possible reaction if they lost, just as Remain complain that Leave had no strategy in place if they won.

Both sides were, at the close of voting, apparently convinced that despite Leave's best efforts, Remain would win.

Their reaction, as we experienced the euphoria of an unexpected victory, was bitter and telling.

You should never have decided that. You're stupid. We'll ignore you for your own good. We need a second referendum. Let's have a legal challenge. The MP's at least will shoot this absurdity down.

So much for free will and respect for the people of this nation.

It was Remain's reaction above all that cemented an opinion that had formed as I looked at other matters of policy in this country.

We live, as do other nations in the west, not in a democracy, but in a democratically elected autocracy.

A Democratically Elected Autocracy

While it may seem that immigration was the only issue, and while Remain painted it as far as possible as a 'racist' issue, it was a symptom of a far deeper issue.

We in the west have inherited the Roman model of government, a hierarchical authority. For all the 'novelty' of the US model as they see it, that distinction is more a matter of marketing than fact.

The US still has a 'supreme figure', praesidens, nominated governor of a province of Rome; and it has a Senate. And it has its Circuses, its Games, in a Colosseum or Superbowl. (Interestingly, the two terms are essentially synonymous, the Colosseum being a 'colossal' amphitheatre or super bowl.

We are constantly told that in a democracy we are a free people. After all, we have elections. Rome had elections too.

And a Roman citizen, very much like an American citizen, was superior simply because he was Roman.

The Rome of history looks a lot like America today, or Britain in her period of Empire, nations which considered themselves superior because they had achieved military and economic superiority over their rivals.

Why is that relevant to us as voters, as citizens?

Contrast that top-down authority, which was overwhelmingly Remain, with the experience of the people.

The principle responsibility of governments in these nations is and was to keep the people quiet. It had its agenda, and if you were one of the great and the good, it was your agenda.

If you weren't, your job was to eat, sleep, and pay your taxes or otherwise be compliant and supportive.

The shock of Remain at the vote's result can be simply explained as the shock of seeing people disobeying those who feel entitled to run our lives.

Is that presumption of theirs legitimate, God-given?

Hardly.

Human Dignity and Free Will

We are born with a natural human dignity. It is present because of what we are, which depending on your philosophy might be a biological individual, a child of God, or an ensouled being.

Regardless of our personal choice of philosophy, how many of us feel we were born to serve others?

Not many I suspect.

There is a very simple premise which does not need to be codified, because it is indeed self-evident, above all.

We have free will.

Whatever you'd care to do in this precise moment is entirely your choice. People may react to it, but you can't be prevented from making that choice.

At the root of the vote then is a question that applies to our relationship to our own government, as much as it applies to the EU:

Were we born to serve another?

The vote said no, and rightly so.

No More Agendas

Everyone who wanted us to stay in had an agenda, whether it was as simple as their wallet, or the liberal agenda of 'culture' in this 'multi-cultural Britain' that they were packing fit to burst, or the Eurocrats with their 'one superstate' agenda.

Everyone had an agenda.

Including, in a sense, Leave, those old white thickos.

We were tired of other people's agendas.

You don't need an agenda to live a good life.

Telling us how to run our lives, both in our own governments, and in the super-state unelected authority of the EU, conflict with that.

When the people voted against the EU, not Europe but the EU political system installed on top of European sovereign governments, they registered a vote that said we no longer trust the EU to be acting in our best interests.

That, to me, is a remarkably rational position.

Lies, Deceit and Exaggeration

Remain's explanation for their defeat is simple. On top of the 'old white thicko' mantra, Leave, Farage and Johnson sold lies, deceit and exaggeration.

Strangely enough, throughout the campaign, I'd say that we saw Cameron, Osborne, the leaders of the EU, US, and world institutions offer little but lies, deceit and exaggerations.

So much so, that it became a personal hobby to shoot down the more popular absurdities on Facebook and LinkedIn.

But really, the campaign was never about the spoken words, never about the pronouncements from the great and the good, or the 'vile' Leave figureheads.

The words were of little account, because the real campaign was very simple:

Do you want to be in charge of your life, or should someone else be?

Hate and Derision

It is remarkable how much hate and denigration Remain are capable of, a side so determined to present Leave as the haters.

While seventeen million Leave voters, more than elect a party to government, are derided as racist, xenophobic thickos, it is Remain who took to the streets in protest, Remain who resorted to name calling, to insults.

Did we see crowds of Leave voters, Paris style, or in echoes of Munich in the thirties, descending on foreign businesses and people?

Hardly. We were all at home, astonished and delighted.

While migrants, Muslims, the French, have been rioting, killing, and bombing across Europe, the worst that someone could come up with for Leave is that apparently there has been some name calling.

And a shop was burned. So there's an idiot out there.

Remain are so determined to deride and hate Leave, that they're incapable of seeing that they're the ones who are emotionally overwrought, angry, and determined to get revenge.

Lack of Trust

The lack of trust in government is a 'deep concern' to politicians.

It should be.

If you want to be free, then you have to eject the masters. There is no excuse for people to be managed. An ideal government would be one that managed the common resources, not the common people.

It is entirely a presumption on the part of people who like being politicians, who like serving in governments and government institutions, that their job is to manage us.

No, their job is to provide a service so that we may go about our lives as we see fit, and provided we don't harm another, that should be all there is to it.

The expansion of 'harm' should be treated with caution, as it has largely become an excuse for ever more intervention.

It may be time for us to think about winding in that presumption, so that government actually serves the people.

Pushing To Leave

Many people served to push the Britons backing Leave to get out and vote, and give Britain its historic victory.

Yes Boris did his part, and Farage has earned a place in democratic history for obliging Cameron to give us the opportunity to vote. Regardless of our opinion of the man, his gift to the British people is unparalleled in modern times, and should be recognised as such by any true lover of democracy.

Which is why he will never receive that accolade from Remain.

Against our betters and masters, the people gave the traditional two fingered salute, and won.

I am or should be one of those betters and masters. A public schoolboy, raised in the Home Counties, six years in the City, the financial district, thirty years in London, I could have voted Remain with London and the Home Counties.

Yet to me the issue was far simpler and far more important than my wallet and potential cost-benefits. When someone decides they have the right to decide my future, I say no, and I will bear the consequences.

For London, if you were a liberal or a financier, basically you voted for your agenda and your wallet, and voted Remain.

Liberals overrode the right to self-determination in their own minds because their agenda fundamentally abhors it. They know better how we should be.

Financiers overrode it because their prime focus on money sets aside anything else.

Leave voters, left and right, even though their wallets might suffer in the short term, voted for something else.

At heart, they voted for other people not telling them what to do. It sounds almost childish. Yet isn't that the essence of freedom, of self-determination?

More importantly, some things are worth suffering the short term consequences for.

As it happens, the sky hasn't fallen on our heads, but even had we been required to suffer recession and turmoil, it would still have been worth it.

Or should we not have fought World War II, because it might have been disturbing to our economy?

Not Yet Enlightened

To a Remainer, it was the height of foolishness to shoot ourselves in the foot, to isolate ourselves from Europe, to deny the huge cultural benefits of immigration, the freedoms and trade benefits we received from a Europe of free movement.

They live in a Shangri La world where ideal humans float in bubbles of light, smiling graciously as we celebrate our common humanity.

That may indeed be what is possible on an enlightened Earth. We are not on an enlightened Earth.

Nor do liberals practice what they preach, when safely in the privacy of their own homes. I'm sure they have locks on the door, just like the rest of us.

Yet publicly, the liberal reverses logic, to say that we should be harmonious and peaceful, so let us push people together so that the get used to that.

The reality is that if you put people with different agendas together, you get disharmony and conflict. We have struggled to reconcile the agendas of left and right, the government as parent versus personal responsibility, and those are only the uncontroversial agendas.

Beyond those, liberals have pushed for an entire lifetime an agenda that says that wherever you come from, your rights to your culture and our homeland supercede our own.

Remain's enthusiasm for policies inimical to our own people encouraged people to finally vote for common sense.

Leavers see real issues, crowding, problems with the provision of services, subjugation of our own rights to emphasise those of newcomers.

Liberals see racism even though the preceding wave of immigration has been white, from Eastern Europe. Fortunately for Remain, we're back to Muslims so they can play the race card again.

Liberals see intolerance, and yes there is, just as they would be intolerant if other people decided that the liberal's home was perfect for their needs, their possessions ready made for selling on for profit.

There is never an excuse to say no in their eyes, so any attempt at reason, at sensible measures, at an appropriate attempt to cope with an already crowded society, is derided. There's always room for more.

Race Agenda

On that other matter, race, there is a similar agenda. I have no problem with race. I do have a problem with politics, and the politics of race has been one of the most divisive influences in the 20th century, and continues to be in the 21st.

I have travelled the world and laughed and spent time with people of all races, and as much as opportunity allowed, indulged in relationships with them, and the two most beautiful women that I sadly did not have the opportunity to engage in a relationship with were a mixed race Asian-Indian/Black American, and a Caribbean Black.

I still wonder what would have happened, had I chosen to fly from Texas to California, instead of Texas to London.

It is not race that divides us, but attitude, and what the politics of race will not allow or recognise is that their determination to push an agenda is divisive and disrespectful of their own people.

We have a right to exist too, and are not here merely to be compliant to their goals. If liberals wish to prove how nice they are, then there are plenty of countries where their services would no doubt be appreciated.

Immigration

The other aspect that was legitimately an issue between Remain and Leave was immigration, and there too the race politicians portrayed any concern about immigration as being an issue of them vs us, an issue of race.

They have done so since the first significant wave of modern immigration began, the most significant transformation of Britain since 1066. As the immigrants were from the West Indies and India, anyone daring to speak up was derided as 'racist' and so the politics of race began.

Only when immigration became white, from Eastern Europe, taking advantage of the EU freedom of movement, did it become possible to discuss immigration as a legitimate issue.

At which point black leaders in Britain spoke up for the need to 'protect British jobs'. The irony was apparently lost on them, for that cry back in the 60's and 70's was meat for the 'race lobby'.

So still the white immigrants came, until job adverts appeared requiring that the applicant must speak Polish, or that a bus driver must be Romanian.

Free Movement

This highlights an issue with the EU agenda. The EU sets 'core' principles that sound reasonable, and may even have been workable as long as the EU remained in its reasonably contained form.

We have free movement. We have had it long before the EU, have had it for most of British history. Internally, there was no material reason to withhold the right. Scots and Welsh were no material threat to the English and vice versa. We are not a uniform people, but rather people from a society with heritage.

Externally, people have long travelled and worked in different countries. Recently, in the contained, limited size, EU, there was a 'western' element, a sense that we were dealing with nations that had histories as equals.

Those nations had peoples who had fought alongside each other in different combinations, trying to keep some sort of balance, trying to avoid the domination of one particular nation.

Typically that has been allying with Germany against France, or allying with France against Germany, as in the Napoleonic and World Wars.

Other than that, people have been travelling in and from Europe, working in and from Europe, for centuries.

27

Cosmopolitan Not Foreign

Where the French holiday in France, we holiday across the world. We trade across the world. Yet we are 'xenophobic little-Englanders'?

Cosmopolitan is interchange with people of other nations, socially and for work. We've been cosmopolitan for centuries.

So it is that by chance my best friend and near constant companion for twenty years or so in London was a German, and I felt deeply embarrassed to watch Saving Private Ryan with six Germans, some of the nicest and most sophisticated people I've met, and compare it to the portrayal of the 'ugly German' on screen.

Thus in the 80's and 90's, London was indeed a cosmopolitan city, a yuppie city, with the Brasserie opposite the Michelin building in South Kensington a fond and popular haunt for brunch on a Sunday. Surrounded by fellow Brits and Europeans, it felt good to be part of a sophisticated crowd.

Foreign is losing your country to another race, another culture, so that you are a minority in your own cities, including boroughs in our capital city, perhaps even in London overall.

Problem With Expansion

Free movement in a community of nations where each already was a successful nation, with a proud history, and a workable economy, was not a big deal. It was just one of those things, a nice touch that meant you didn't have to slow down at the France/Belgium border to show your passport.

Then the EU changed the game.

It sought in its hubris ever greater power, ever greater stature, so that it could call itself a worthy rival to the US, a farcical comparison frankly, but let us not dwell on that aspect.

The EU is a numbers game. With the fall of the Soviet Union, both it and the US hurried to include the newly 'liberated' nations into Nato. All those nations would then require 'Nato compatible' equipment.

The consequences of actions are rarely properly thought out, or more disturbingly, they were simply disregarded.

It didn't matter if Russia felt threatened as Nato expanded right up to Russia's border. So what? They were dead, ancient history. Look at the potential for arms sales.

The EU wanted those nations too. More people, bigger numbers, they could point to their 'growing power' in the world.

It was an illusion, and remains an illusion.

But in the process of pursuing it they crossed a threshold. The newly acquired nations were not rich nations, had no shared heritage with the western nations, had indeed spent most of a lifetime failing while the west grew rich. The eastern nations could only look on, surviving as best they could, while the west flourished and grew indolent, indulgent, self-absorbed.

While the west were feasting, the east were starving, not absolutely perhaps, but it didn't take a degree to see where life was good and life was easy.

In a world where borders were recognised and controlled that might not have mattered.

In a world where the nations were relatively similar in wealth, status and outlook, that might not have mattered.

Once the EU absorbed nations who were relatively impoverished compared to our own, combine that with free movement and the result was inevitable.

The EU was like a submarine with its hatch jammed open by choice. The water poured in.

Given the choice of staying in their failed economies, their failed societies so recently abandoned by Russia, free to do their own thing, they did it: they left in huge numbers to find work in the wealthy west.

Who could blame them?

Any hope of a gradual transition to western standards of wealth was set aside.

If free movement had been a nice convenience in a stable group of nations, it had now being transformed into a gateway to Shangri La for people who were quick to take advantage.

If the EU had intended to maintain the integrity of its nations on behalf of the people, it was remarkably inept in not seeing this coming.

Or, to those who promote the EU, a homogenous Europe with little people shared around equally, there just isn't a problem.

Undermining the Race Agenda

There was however one key thing about these immigrants which finally allowed something extraordinary to happen. They were white, so finally we could discuss immigration without being accused of being racists. The liberals wanted to use it, but even they struggled with that one.

The CRE, the Commission for Racial Equality, had been the outspoken supporter of immigrants and lost no opportunity to castigate Britain and Britons for its failure to do more for immigrants. It was race, race, race, as its name suggests.

Now, confronted with widespread white immigration, Blacks and Asian minorities protested, and the CRE was forced to rebrand itself.

It is now, I believe, the 'Equality and Human Rights Commission'. No matter who you are, we've got you covered.

The one good thing about the Eastern European rush for jobs was that at least it showed the hypocrisy of the race politicians. It wasn't about race, it was about jobs and life in Britain, just as we'd always said it was.

Disregard and Disrespect

There is a disturbing element to the naivety, as it may seem to be at first glance, about free movement.

What if it isn't naivety, but design?

What if the EU masters, the EU architects, don't mind where people are, or worse, actually think that the mass influx of immigrant labour from Eastern Europe is a good thing?

As long as they have the numbers to push in the face of their American colleagues and competitors, it shows that the EU has clout, has weight.

Any problems can be dealt with at the local level. If Poland wants to migrate to the UK, that will simply show up as increased economic vitality in the UK, and indeed that is precisely what did show up, and most people I know will say 'Thank God for hard working Eastern Europeans'. They are fed up with the poor quality and high prices of British non-workmanship.

Call me stupid, but eventually having all work done by Eastern Europeans and no work done by the British leaves us with an unskilled, unemployable workforce.

Well, that's what welfare is for.

Mandated Devolution

Thus it is that the country that transformed the world with the Industrial revolution has now been engaged in post-industrial-devolution. For a brief moment perhaps, at the dawn of the welfare state, there was balance, as people recognised that working hard all your life shouldn't be an inescapable punishment with no safety net.

The Welfare State was born and retirement set at 65 (men) for a simple reason: very few people lived that long. Women tend to live longer, but their retirement age was 60. Go figure.

Now we have a life expectancy of around 80, and that's the average, so that many will survive till 90, even 100.

We are bankrupting the nation, which really means we are putting ever more of a burden on the taxpayer, essentially the middle class, with no proposal as to how to get away from basic demographics.

It isn't the fault of the middle class that people are living longer, but there is no one else who's going to pay the bills.

Cheap labour undercutting locals, burgeoning welfare, an aging population. It isn't looking pretty, except for business. Fortunately, politicians are on their side.

And then, Syria

Humans are incredibly adaptable and resilient, so we will survive whatever our masters throw at us.

Probably.

Syria however has added another dimension, though this can more properly be traced to 9/11 and its aftermath, comprising Afghanistan, Iraq, Isis and Syria.

'Closed borders' is the new rallying cry as the migrant crisis evolves, and that is hardly surprising.

Except it wasn't the first call that made it out as the crisis grew.

'We welcome you', went out from Merkel, and the grateful migrants of the East responded.

It was a remarkably inept call, or rather it may have been what Merkel believed and stood for, but it hasn't taken long for the Germans and other Europeans to realise the folly of the words and the seriousness of the crisis.

Fences are going up across Europe, countries are refusing to take in migrants, and Merkel has even come out against the Burkha. Amazing what can happen in a few short weeks.

Migrants not Refugees

Quick reminder and definition: a refugee flees to the first safe country or region and stops, then wishes to go home. A migrant stops without wishing to go home or wishes to go further.

The images that were so derided when displayed by Farage are no more than fact.

More to the point, Britons are far from alone in being concerned about the consequences. Entire governments in Europe have set themselves against accepting these migrants.

Images show lines of fit young men sadly unable to fight for their homeland, unable to defend their women and children, but more than capable of using their phones (where did they get them?) as they surge into western Europe, the Shangri La with its wealth and open doors.

Nor do they stop in Greece, or Italy, or Hungary, or France or even Germany. Why on earth someone from Syria would want to go to Sweden escapes me. Lovely country but cold in winter. Yet that is apparently a hot destination.

As are we.

Apparently We're Special

It's not enough to be in La Belle France, a thousand miles or whatever it is from Syria or Eastern Europe. No, the last twenty miles, the one with the pesky channel in the way, are the critical ones, and the 'refugees' will riot, stop traffic, ride trains, walk through tunnels, hide in lorries, or hijack vehicles obliging drivers to take them across that final barrier to Shangri La.

Whatever we have, it must be of inestimable value, even by comparison to France.

I frankly cannot conceive of anything intrinsic to the UK that is so superior or more desirable.

Yes, we have the international language, but really, that's hardly a big deal.

Yes, I think we're a wonderful nation on the whole, fair minded, tolerant, but you'd have to get to know us to know that. How well do these migrants know us?

Whatever is so utterly compelling, it far exceeds anything that France has, and I'd love for someone to tell me what it is.

Unless of course it's a simple as wealth and welfare.

A Crowded Nation

Here in the South Central Enland, with forty million people, we're already the most crowded western region on the planet and the ninth most crowded region on the planet, the other eight being essentially in India and China.

I do not recall ever any government saying that the purpose of our nation was to make it the most crowded place on earth.

An 'international' nation for three thousand years, since the Celts first immigrated from Gaul to mingle with the nomadic natives, we have been faced with hundreds of thousands, millions indeed, of people who did not bring with them schools, hospitals, cars or transport, but relied instead on our supplying them.

The 'enormous cultural and economic benefit' per migrant has been calculated to be a few pounds, when all services are netted out.

I get that people want to come here.

That doesn't mean we have to let them.

It's a matter of choice. For one brief moment, we were given that choice, and we said no.

Irrevocable Change

For a lifetime, the choice of government has never been centrally about immigration, and yet there is no more fundamental issue. It has rather been about our wallets, the right to take from them and the degree to which that should be possible.

Immigration was a war fought in the media against the British people. We were never given a vote, never a choice. It was a policy imposed upon us.

By 1973, the native British birth rate had dropped to breakeven. The native British population stalled, at 56 million people.

Now at 65 million people, all growth since then has been by immigration and children of immigrants.

Simple arithmetic, from 56 million people in 1973 to 65 million today, gives a figure of 9 million immigrants, or about 14%. It is interesting to not that the figure coincides with a figure of 13% seen in a piece by an American source.

No government can now be elected without appealing to the minorities. In certain boroughs of London, they are no longer even minorities. In less than a lifetime, liberals and politicians have imposed a policy by determined effort that has completely transformed the nature of our nation, without regard to the desires, will or right to decide of the British people.

I do not hate anyone of another race, but I do hate people who impose their will on others 'for their own good'.

In my experience, what is decided by others to be good for me, is usually good for them. We see the argument all the time: it's called advertising.

You won't really get a girl with that aftershave, but they will get your money.

For the proponents of immigration, there were clear benefits, as we've noted: cheap labour for business, and 'nice' credentials for liberals. All those poor people now living in free and ideal Britain.

The liberals and politicians have fundamentally transformed this nation without ever bothering to ask whether it was a transformation we required or desired.

Simple demographics says that we will someday be a minority in our own land, not just our cities. Let us hope that the dominant people then are as generous and liberal to us, as our politicians have been to them.

Thank You Remain

Remain were the best advert for Leave that Leave could have wished for.

Sir Bob Geldof, if he didn't already have a knighthood, we'd have to give him one. Two fingers to British fisherman says it all about the world the 'liberals' live in.

Cameron, and self-harming Britons. Adolescents who are mentally disturbed, a mantra that Remain have kept going in their old, white, thicko refrain.

Corbyn - did Corbyn do anything during the campaign?

Blair, Brown, Major - that would be Tony Blair of WMD fame, would it?

Osborne and his 'I'll punish you' budget. Interesting how quiet he got, like a schoolboy whose friend has been naughty and been kicked out, but he thought he got away with it. No matter, Cameron will sort him with a nice gong.

Honorary Remainers, given their intent, but fantastic ambassadors for Leave, were of course Merkel, Juncker, Hollande. Every threat was worth a handy sum of votes. Since no one has done a demographic on that, we'll have to just imagine the numbers, but given the pleasure of seeing threat after threat coming out of Europe, I feel certain they were a major contribution to Leave victory.

And if that reminds you of a certain tyre advert from a long time ago…

Of course the biggest weakness in Remain was that they simply had nothing to say.

They spoke, but to no particular effect, and their claims as to principle were absurd and off the mark, while of course their dire prognostications of doom made no sense then and have since been disproven.

In fact, as of this revision, August 2016, 'experts' are now having to grudgingly admit we can do well out, out of the EU.

Maybe they feel an urge to face reality, necessarily so, if they ever want to be taken seriously again.

Overall, I believe the problem was that Remain simply assumed that of course it's better to be in Europe, and then struggled to come up with any particular justification as to why.

As ever, we're not leaving Europe, just the EU.

Test your liberal credentials

Let us take a scenario and see whether liberals are really that different.

Take a well-off Remainer, with their enlightened partner and two adorable children, in their four bedroomed house with perhaps eight rooms.

Knock on their door, and present them with a family that has come to Britain believing it to be a Shangri La of opportunity, wealth and free health care. We need to house them, so we've chosen this Remainer family to do so.

They have four bedrooms, eight rooms. There is plenty of room.

How will they react, especially when they hear that they have no choice in the matter?

This is our decision. They will take that family.

The Remainers are a very nice family, so reluctantly (or willingly) the Remainers take the necomers in, assign them a bedroom, and carry on with their lives.

Although there are two adult and two child immigrants, the Remainers nevertheless feel that as it is their house, a house they worked towards and paid for, it's not unreasonable to only give the new family one bedroom, instead of two.

The children turn out to be a bit noisier than expected, and the adults are polite but find it disrespectful if the Remainer family intrude on their prayers.

No matter, being a good liberal family, Mrs Remainer goes out of her way to ensure that the new family understands how excited she is that they are there.

It's not what she'd have hoped for, but they'll get by.

Then there's another knock on the door. Another family requires housing.

There's a bit more of a kerfuffle this time, as the Remainers point out they are already housing one immigrant family, but we sternly point out that they cannot object. These people are an important contribution to the diversity of our nation and we want to provide housing for them.

There's also a problem because the new family insists that the children must not stay in the same bedroom as the adults, so they will require two bedrooms. With one bedroom given to the first family, and the Remainer parents having another, that means no bedroom for the Remainer children.

That definitely does not go down well with the Remainer children, so the mother has to explain to them that the new people are good people and its their civic duty as inclusive citizens to ensure that their wishes are accomodated.

Things are a bit fraught, as the first newcomers resent that the second family get two bedrooms, while the second family goes about their day quite happily, if not as tidily as Mrs Remainer might like.

The Remainer children become surly, which Mrs Remainer finds disappointing, and she finds she has to castigate them more, instilling in them the lessons of inclusiveness, that we are all equal, that we are all welcome.

She also asks her husband to deal with the first family who are using the children's play room for prayers, and who have pushed the toys to one side and installed an altar of some sort.

He reluctantly does so and the first family become angry at the intrusion into their space. The police are called, Mr Remainer is given a lecture, and the first newcomers are victorious. Mr Remainer must adapt to them.

There is a knock on the door. We have a third family, they've just arrived, don't speak the language, but they will need accomodation.

The first family are already in one room, and the second family refuse to give up their second bedroom. Mrs Remainer tentatively wonders whether the Remainers should give up their bedroom, but Mr Remainer offers some robust Anglo Saxon reply to that suggestion.

Apologising to the third family, Mrs Remainer clears out the dining room, though the dining table turns out to be useful for changing nappies, as the third family have four infant children.

They smile a lot and settle in, but there's a problem when the third family start storing their dirty washing in the play room where the first family have created a prayer room.

There is another knock at the door.

Keep going until there are eleven families plus the Remainers.

That is how many families are sometimes, it is said, crammed into houses in London by unscrupulous landlords.

After how many families would the Remainers rebel, have a breakdown, abandon the house entirely?

If any Remainer thinks that scenario is nonsense, that of course they'd accept eleven other families in their home, then I'd like to see that in practice.

If they say that's not our problem, that's the government's problem then we get to the nub of the issue.

Liberals like feel-good agendas.

They don't like having to live with the consequences.

When more realistic Leavers who have to live with the consequences raise an objection, the feel-good liberals can point the finger and say how bad we are, how much we owe it to these people, how we should be inclusive, but they still go home to live in their comfortable isolation of their perfectly managed homes.

Remainers understand the concept of space, of choice, of limitations, of conflict, of resources.

They just don't like to recognise them when they conflict with their agenda.

For decades, fifty, sixty years, we've had the liberal agenda foist upon us.

We were never given a say, a vote, a choice.

Finally, thanks overwhelmingly to one man, Farage, we were given a choice.

And against all the odds, we said no, out, leave.

It's not that we hate foreigners. As a world traveller, that is an absurd accusation. It's that we hate liberals who think they know better than us, and so override common sense and legitimate concerns.

Free Movement and the Migrant Crisis

The current migrant crisis is really three different crises.

The first is that of internal EU migration from the poorer nations of Eastern Europe to the West.

The second is external migration from Africa in particular, across to Spain and Italy.

The third is the fallout from the Syrian conflict.

We have little or no natural affinity for or relationship with the nations of Eastern Europe. Under Soviet domination for decades, their economies are such that their people are making an entirely rational choice to head west, to where they perceive the wealth to be.

It is a symbol of the EU's greed and hubris that it expanded enthusiastically to absorb these new candidates, nations that would add numbers to the EU's claim to be a global power.

The leaders' disregard for the impact on us is telling, likewise its impact on Russia, who were less than happy to find the EU and Nato on its very border.

Some point to Poland, whose pilots are rightly honoured for their determination to continue the fight in Britain, afer their country had fallen.

It was a fight to free Europe and their country in particular, not a struggle to establish an economic foothold in Britain.

The non-EU migration from Africa, again seeking to flee poverty, is less an issue for us, as they cross the Mediterranean to land in Italy or Spain.

The Syrian 'refugee' crisis is remarkably free of refugees, people who stop in the first safe country, and is instead strongly characterised as fit young men, opportunistically headed for Germany, Sweden or Britain.

Nor has the behaviour of these Muslim migrants been comfortable to behold. Even without Isis, assaults and rape have become a near daily staple, the latter issue being one that is particularly uncomfortable for the liberals: who should they support, the foreign migrant or the domestic (local) woman?

The media have responded by either ignoring the news, or re-branding the assaults, especially killings, so that you have to read in the small print that the assailant shouted 'Allah Akhbar' as he attacked.

That might be a clue.

A Disturbing Principle

All of the various elements of the migrant crisis are compounded in their effect by the EU's directive on internal free movement of people, including the right to live and work where you like, and essentially to be treated as a generic citizen wherever you find yourself.

This directive is one of the 'founding principles' of the modern EU according to European politicians, a statement which astonished me when I read it.

For it to be an experiment, a desire, something which would be nice, is one thing. To declare it as a 'founding principle' is something else. It gives it VIP status, up there with, and apparently superior to, sovereignty, self-determination, the right to be and have a nation.

It is far more than simply not needing to show your passport as you travel from from France to Germany. It is a conceptualisation of an EU superstate with homogenous people flowing around like ingredients swirling in a dish, free to serve whatever interest is most efficient and profitable in our glorious and ever expanding EU.

To set that as a 'core principle' is disturbing indeed.

It says that a people's will is of no account, that people from the poorer nations will flow inevitably to the richer, that those richer nations are then obliged to accept and provide for those people, who ultimately have one role to play: cheap labour.

It is a side of globablisation that I'd prefer not to have to confront, because it really does show a cynical disregard for the people by our betters and masters in Brussels in London.

It is one thing to enjoy convenient travel to a holiday destination. It is quite another to knowingly insist that the people in a nation are of no account, that convenience and efficiency for business, for profit, are the be-all and end-all for the EU.

I believe in business. I do not believe in business at the expense of our own people.

We did not need the EU to visit France, or Germany, or Italy before the EU existed. Nor do we need the EU to visit the US, or Africa, Asia, the Middle East.

So the EU's 'freedom of movement' is primarily directed to allow uncontrolled movement, movement that among other things weakens the trade unions, the existing labour force.

Free Movement really means Cheap Labour Migration

The Problem With Principles

Even if it had been something desirable, then the problem with setting it up as a 'core principle' is simple: it becomes something to defend, something to avoid giving up at all costs.

It becomes a door jammed open. When the scale of the current migration became clear, a prompt and decisive response was called for.

We got it, in the shape of million-migrant Merkel, and her 'come on in, the door is open'. Her call handily exacerbated the crisis, entirely in line with the motivation behind free movement, the desire to pull in cheap labour to the wealthier nations.

Where others saw a concern, and their concerns were duly shown to be legitimate, with riots, killings, bombings, rape to follow, she saw cheap labour.

When the fences started going up, that is when the EU leaders started talking about free movement as a 'core principle'. Labelling it as such gave the leaders the excuse not to do anything.

And that is the problem with principles, that they don't sit well with common sense; or they get cited to justify action or inaction that are ultimately unreasonable.

A principle that is aligned with common sense will stand you in good stead, such as the right and desire for self-determination, which is a natural expression of free will.

Nations and governments that were more wedded to reality and common sense acted decisively. Fences went up, and declarations were clear: no migrants for us.

Hungary took a robust lead in such, and the contrast between the actions and declarations of Hungary, and the inaction of France and Britain over Calais, are telling.

The real benefit of the migrant crisis, if we can call it a benefit, is that it revealed just how wedded our EU masters are to their superstate/globalisation/cheap labour ideal.

It made our decision on Brexit all the more appropriate.

Right and Left Aligned

I am in many ways a right wing conservative, a libertarian conservative, someone who thinks that people are entitled to experience life to the maximum of survival, comfort and exploration.

Yet is that really right wing?

I believe that our sense of integrity, our self-determination, our free will, are beyond left and right.

If I point out the weakening effect of free movement on labour and labour unions, then I am not a fan of such unions, but I do respect that people, individuals, have to get on with their lives and deserve an opportunity to thrive and flourish.

That is difficult to do if you are being constantly undercut by a low-cost labour force.

That we should struggle to resolve a balance between integrity of the business and the dignity of the employees who create that business is one thing, where it concerns our own people, our own citizens.

To be part of a supranational agreement to jam the doors open, against the interests of our own people, but as a handy fix for big business, is quite another.

Not Very Socialist

Yet here's the strange thing: the socialists, the liberals, the intelligentsia, the Guardian indeed, were and are rabidly 'pro Europe'... pro immigration, pro cheap labour. Aren't Labour supposed to be for the people?

Ordinary people, left and right, including a great many Labour voters, voted to Leave, to restrict immigration, to slow down and sort out this cheap-labour, pro-business directive.

That looks eminently sensible.

It stands in stark contrast with their betters and masters in the Labour party. These are people who are supposed to have spent a lifetime defending the British people, the British worker, against the excesses of the bosses, as they see it.

For them to be determinedly Remain, pro-Europe, pro immigration, pro cheap Labour, is astonishing, unless of course there's an overriding loyalty to something else.

Offhand, I don't know what that is: money, power, a liberal agenda, being part of a club?

I do know that politicians of both parties, the people supposed to represent the voters, were giving very dodgy advice. Fortunately we ignored it.

Cameron and Corbyn

I understand Cameron being a presumptuous, smug, superior being. He's an Eton Tory, he's supposed to be.

I disliked him long before Brexit, never trusted him, and in the vote, his disregard and disdain for the British people finally revealed the man that I'd instinctively disliked, but without being able to pin down the reason for it.

I may be a natural Tory, but I was glad to vote against the will of our political masters, and I use the term 'master' with some sense of irony, skepticism, even derision, particularly in the light of their recent behaviour during the campaign.

I get that side of things.

I don't get the Labour side of things.

How can politicians supposed to be representing the people, be so determined to jam the door open against them, a door the people have very sensibly, if belatedly, called to be closed?

Back to the Motherland

I have to hark back to the roots of the 'homeland' of socialism, back to the USSR, back to the motherland, to find a similar loyalty to the State over the People.

I thought all that was over.

We won, didn't we?

Capitalism over communism, free markets over controlled markets, freedom over control.

Why does Remain look so much like a determined wish to live in the good old days, when central authority was in charge?

Is it really as simple as that, because after all, isn't that exactly what the vote was? It was a choice between a yes to central power in Brussels, overriding the UK state; or no to central power in Brussels, putting the power back where it should be, in the UK.

In the light of which, how can anyone legitimately be for Remain? It beggars belief that people can truly want to opt for central authority again.

Central Power, Again?

It didn't work for Russia.

The Soviet Union finally got broken up, the countries freed, and they of course were hungrily lapped up by the EU, giving us of course the internal migrant crisis of free movement.

It didn't work in Germany, which got out of hand, and we had to slap it down.

It didn't work in France, which got out of hand, and we had to slap it down.

What is it about people who want to see ever greater power vested in a single authority, that they won't give it a rest?

And why is it that once again France and Germany are pushing for it, and more disturbing still, that our own politicians are supporting them?

The marketing is slicker, the implementation non-violent, but the intention and outcome are the same: dominion and control.

Thanks, but no thanks.

Common Cause

That big business wants to enjoy cheap labour is easy to understand, though it is hardly laudable when it comes at the expense of our own people.

That politicians should push so determinedly for that, given that they're supposed to be representing the people, is more disturbing.

Unless of course, they're elected by people, but that doesn't mean they're loyal to the people who elected them.

We voted, left and right, to leave the EU, the political system on top of Europe. Maybe out of the we can recognise that we have a common cause that we may care to pay more attention to.

We do the work, the politicians and their sponsors, the hyper-wealthy and big business, get the benefit.

The Hamster Wheel

This is the illusion at the heart of the US and the West (Europe), perhaps elsewhere also, but it is particularly a feature of the US.

'The Land of Opportunity.'

Work hard, play hard, look at these people who have achieved wealth, and who give something back by donating money to charity. Look at Mark Zuckerberg and his adorable selfies on Facebook.

You could be him.

With the right attitude, hard work, you could be in the stratosphere along with him.

It is the great lie of modern western society.

It is a conclusion I have come to, the more I have researched what actually goes on behind the scenes in government and industry. The more I looked into 9/11, the armaments industry, and our subsequent fourteen years of war, the more I've appreciated that politics and industry go hand in hand, as it seems also, does war.

There are essentially four bands in any western society, five if we include the political class.

There is the destitute/welfare band, people who either by inclination or capacity are unwilling or unable to fend effectively for themselves.

There is the blue collar/working class band, people who do menial to professional jobs, the kind of people who get their hands dirty for modest or decent pay, for whom getting a roof over their heads of their own is a worthwhile accomplishment.

There is the white collar/middle class band, people who do professional office jobs, the lawyers and accountants, the financiers who are solid but not stars, the doctors and surgeons, the pilots.

Then there is the stratosphere, the people who achieve escape velocity, or in this case the wealth to escape need or want, the business leaders, tycooons, icons.

The hamster wheel is the means by which these societies operate, and it revolves (so to speak) around the first three tiers. Simply put, individuals, predominantly the white collar/middle class but also the blue collar/working class, pay 90% of the government's budget.

That, to me, is an extraordinarily high figure.

Don't most of us work for businesses, for corporations?

Do you feel like the wealthy patron of a business or a corporation? How come then, if you don't, that we're paying 90%, and the corporations are paying somewhat less than 10%?

Someone's got a nice deal.

I wonder who arranged that? Perhaps the same people who then arrange for our money, that of left and right taxpayers alike, to be distributed to buy the votes to get elected.

Yes, it provides welfare and public services too, but the real question is why ordinary people, who don't have the leisure to give up work, pay 90% of the bills for government, while commerce, especially big business, and the wealthy are free to find the most efficient tax havens.

Did I mention that modern society sounds a lot like Rome?

Above the world of mortals, those who go to work, pay bills, pay their taxes, manage a holiday or two maybe, celebrate Christmas, then start again, is another world.

The stratosphere is a world which begins perhaps in wealth measured in the tens of millions. However it really kicks in at the level of hundreds of millions, billions. The world today even has its first trillionaire.

And those are just the individuals. Corporations of course take such size for granted.

The stratosphere is a very tax-efficient world. The US titans soak up a billion dollars in sales in the UK and pay a derisory 1%, 10 million dollars, in tax.

Sourced in China, sold in the UK, profits to the US.

I always find it amusing when I hear the US complain about China milking the US. They certainly don't complain that Google, Amazon, et al, are milking us.

And I'm not immune to the karma, if you like, that the Empire that once did that to India, is now qthe fall guy in the same scheme for the US.

Or that big business now outsources all their IT and call centre work to India.

The point is that while the politicians have been distracting us with left-worker vs right-worker, the western world revolves around the people it has always revolved around, the movers and shakers, big business and extremely wealthy people.

Coincidence

The 'free movement of labour and capital' serves big business and extremely wealthy people. The governments and politicians serve big business and extremely wealthy people, before becoming moderately wealthy themselves, as Tony Blair has so elegantly demonstrated.

It is sold to us as globalisation, but to the WalMart worker in the US, the worker who sees Polish workers taking their job in the UK, it doesn't feel like a brave new world, a world of opportunity.

It feels like someone taking the piss.

Or taking the mickey, if that's more familiar.

Maybe it's time to stop paying quite so much attention to left and right, and time to start paying attention to the other them and us, those in power, and those who pay for it.

We came together somewhat to vote to Leave.

We don't have to disband back to our sides. We may, if we wish, find a common cause, a common purpose that suits us, rather than other people's agendas.

Integrity

There is a reason they put bulkheads on a ship, a reason that you have skin: it places a barrier against unrestricted migration, of water in each case.

Integrity of the body, integrity of the ship, relies upon restrictions, so that changes are moderated.

Liberals have bought into their own propaganda without enough thought. They have no regard for the integrity of our nation or its people.

Human beings, if they are to be respected, are entitled to operate in a realm where they can self-determine their lives, contributing as appropriate, without undue duress.

There is little economic gain when someone is imported to take a job for low pay and has to have services provided for them from scratch. That makes it harder for a local to make their own contribution, someone who then also takes a lower wage, needs more services in support, more welfare.

So when the EU continues its agenda, telling us what people should do, what nations must do, and how we must adhere to their core principles for the greater good, a quiet resentment seethes, even as our liberals tell us we're wrong, and our wallet-heads, our bankers enjoy their opportunity to make hay.

Ultimately, why Leave wanted to win was down to an elite telling us how to think, telling us we were wrong to have any thoughts of restrained population, of sensible rules, of respect for our own culture.

The refrain was constant, always that we must do more to be 'inclusive', do more to respect different cultures, in complete disregard to our own society, our own needs.

Nor even did everyone who came here want to be inclusive, to be part of our secular society.

What they wanted, what they liked, was our remarkable tolerance, tolerance not granted in their home countries. That tolerance, far from seeing them drop their home culture, encouraged them to insist upon it.

It's a matter of opinion whether it's a healthy sign that young 'Britons' go off to war to fight against us.

Personally, I don't believe it is.

We're paying the price for decisions made decades ago and assiduously reinforced ever since. Perhaps it's time that we paid attention and insisted on policies that serve us, not other people.

The vote was an excellent beginning.

Why did we win?

We've explained or suggested somewhat why we wanted to win, but when nobody believed it to be possible, why did we win?

We shouldn't have.

The list of people and institutions arrayed against us was immense:

Cameron, Osborne, Corbyn

The two major parties, Tory and Labour

Former Prime Ministers, left and right: Blair, Brown, Major

Foreign leaders: Hollande, Merkel, Juncker, Obama

The Bank of England, World Bank, UK Government, all with their doom and gloom statistics

US Corporates (interfering in a sovereign nation's politics, no surprise from the home of the CIA)

The liberals: Sir Bob Geldof, JK Rowling

The entrepreneurs; Sir Richard Branson

And Jo Cox.

Even against all the titans, it actually seemed we might win, so much so that at a wedding complete with bells, I imagined the same bells ringing out over England on VE day, Victory over Europe, on pretty much the seventieth anniversary of an earlier VE day.

And then I went home and read about Jo Cox.

And read about Jo Cox.

And read about Jo Cox.

Every day, article after article: how Jo Cox would have wanted us to vote Remain.

With Remain on the rails, overnight the polls turned, and it was Leave that was behind.

Our historic opportunity washed away by a lone gunman.

Not the first time that a lone gunman had changed events, so much so, and so neatly with Remain behind, that if this was the US, I'd be looking carefully at the story behind the story.

But this is the UK. We don't do that sort of thing, do we?

And so I watched with increasing bitterness as the future of our nation was decided by one woman's tragedy.

A personal tragedy became a national tragedy, and anyone daring to suggest that the issue was bigger than one death would be derided as heartless.

Then we went to the polls.

A strange thing happened after the polls closed.

The Jo Cox stories disappeared, and have never resurfaced. Not even one comment has surfaced that I have seen to the effect that 'Jo Cox would have wanted a second referendum'.

As all the Remain politicians stood piously or sat piously in the House of Commons, they all knew that the defeat staring them in the face had been averted. Jo Cox had saved them, and they knew it.

And so did we.

Boris Johnson admitted that Remain had most likely won.

Farage conceded defeat shortly after the polls closed.

None of us, Leave supporters, I believe truly believed we could win.

We had done something extraordinary, resisted all the big guns.

But the liberals had emoted, and polling day was her birthday.

You couldn't make it up.

If you had to choose a victim, there would never have been a better one.

And so with the polls closed, we waited.

I tried to get into the spirit of things, renting Branagh's Henry V from Amazon, but it didn't really suit.

I tried Waterloo, and that went much better, and the hours passed.

We knew, we'd been told, that if Sunderland was 56% we had a chance.

Boney turned his eyes to the sky.

The Old Guard was falling back.

Against the odds, with Blucher turning up in the early evening, Britain had survived.

Napoleon was vanquished.

Britain and Prussia had prevailed. Europe was saved.

I went for a smoke.

And the first results came in.

Earlier that day, as I'd had to nip out, the heavens had opened.

At Agincourt, the mud that day slowed the knights to a slog. It saw them slaughtered, taking knives through their visors, those that survived the arrows.

At Waterloo, the mud that day delayed the start of Napoleon's attack for hours.

Were these storms a sign?

I hoped so, not with any faith, but just as a hope, the slightest thought that despite everything, Britons might have recovered from the shock of Jo Cox, and made a decision based on their future.

I sat down, coming back from having my smoke.

Sunderland, 61%.

I couldn't believe it.

My God, we were in with a chance.

I never moved for hours from that point.

As results changed percentages, I took snapshots of the screen.

I saw Gbraltar, 95% Remain, and felt a sense of betrayal.

Who protected them from Spain, us or the EU?

I watched Scotland turn yellow, 60:40 for Remain, basically.

I felt anger at the thought that a close run thing might be decided by the Scots.

I searched for numbers for populations, breaking it down to the list I cited, England, Wales, Scotland,

Northern Ireland, and London. I parsed out England ex-London and London.

I realised that London and Scotland could be a nuisance, could sway a narrow margin, but it was down to England essentially, but would be best if we could be supported by someone.

And Wales matched us, blow for blow, stood beside us, blue after blue. I never felt such affection for that rain-soaked rugged land.

As I did the math, and watched Scotland, I realised that she had shot her bolt. The results came early, and they were heavily in favour of the EU.

At 62:38, a 12 point lead in Scotland, versus a 3 point lead 53:47 in England, Scotland punched four times her weight, giving her population of 5 million, the weight of 20 million. Something to consider when it comes to the issue of Scotland interfering in English/British politics, and under the current leader, Sturgeon, interference is definitely the name of the game.

The overall result dropped to 49:51 against. Then recovered to 50:50.

England though was turning solidly blue, result after result, even the first couple of London results. We were heading up to 53:47.

And then London and the Home Counties started to fill up, and I saw that accursed yellow.

My kin, the yuppies, the middle class, the liberals, the politicians, and the London with its boroughs more immigrant than native-British, a city of our future, as our liberals liked to say, turned against us, and for the EU.

I felt ashamed, betrayed, and glad that my vote had counted in a district that was blue, for Leave.

Did they understand nothing of freedom, of self-determination, of the right to determine our own future?

Apparently not, and as we have learned, nor it seems do they understand or respect democracy.

.

Once Scotland was done, with so much of England to come, the numbers said that even London could not sway the issue.

I didn't believe it though until we were down to a couple of boroughs outstanding in London, but by then the news channels were starting to acknowledge it as real.

Leave had won.

Against all the establishment in the UK, in Europe, in the US, Britons had had their say.

Achieving a historic victory against the EU, to London, to Cameron and Corbyn.

Left and right, we said we want our lives back.

And within hours, after all the short-lived euphoria, we were to learn Remain's answer.

No.

It wasn't enough to have a clear and decisive result. Every means was to be brought to bear to diminish the result, to say it wasn't enough, to demand a 2nd referendum.

They never thought, never dreamed, that they could actually lose.

Yet they did, and now Remain wanted its revenge.

It wanted the result overturned.

They were outraged.

A sad day for Britain. Our children's futures destroyed by old white thickos.

For the Leave voters who thought they'd won a historic victory, they found they had to start all over again, fighting to counter the bitter losers, who'd rather overturn democracy than accept the wrong result.

The story continues, day by day, but that at least for now, is how it felt to be a Leave voter, and what I believe we were voting for.

And by the way, a touching moment:

On Leave.EU, chatting, amazed as the results came in, we were not left and right, but Britons, and then one women self-declared to be black, and I said that after all the vitriol directed at us as 'bigoted, right wing, racist, isolationist, xenophobic, little-Englanders', it was lovely to have her there.

And it was.

Reply in Support of a Leaver

A young man off whom I'd just bought a Mini acknowledged that he was a Leaver, and that 95% of his colleagues (financial) were being quite aggressive on discovering that he'd voted Leave, and he was wondering if he was missing something.

This was my reply.

It addresses a lot of the bullet point objections that we would see in the media and online in postings.

It was:

Those with an agenda and those who love their wallets are blind to a number of things:

a)   We said no to a bunch of unelected autocrats. We did not say we were going to take the UK into the middle of the Atlantic and sink her

b)   Nothing has to change beyond a simple 'non', or a more English 'how fascinating' when Hr Juncker tries to tell the UK what to do

c)   It is ONLY if the EU wish to punish us that there is any risk of damage to our trade. German car makers are not going to want to cut their noses off

d)   A great deal of the hysteria is simply because the great and the good are horrified that the great unwashed have remembered something they've forgotten or never understood: we are Britain, a free and independent nation, and anyone who thought they could sign that away for their wallet was mistaken.

e)   We voted to leave a political system not a continent. Euro MP's also have this conceit they refer to Europe or Project Europe not the EU. It is classic spin. Europe will still be 20.1 miles away as ever. The EU will be a million miles away, as ever.

f)   We do NOT need to go cap in hand to the EU for trade. They are a small proportion of our trade, and Europe is massively dependent on our trade in return, more so in fact I suspect. After all, what do we really sell these days?

g)   This vote removes material threats from the EU table, some of which are imminent and the consequences clear:

h) — taking our own army from our control, the most fundamental protector of our identity and right to exist

i) — taking our police from our control, ditto

j) — implementing an EU tax regime — raising taxes and control are the defining elements of a state

k) — accepting Turkey as a member, the first majority Islam nation — see Istanbul today

l) The 'old white thickos' that won this vote have done a great service for this country in doing what Britain does, protecting its people, participating in Europe, protecting Europe from its own folly

m) We defeated Spanish interference, including a back door attempt through Mary Queen of Scots, appropriately enough, a long time ago

n) More recently we twice defeated a 'unified Europe' under Napoleon, twice under Germany

o) We are at peace in Europe not because of the EU but because we devastated Germany and gave them such a bloody nose, they had no desire to see that repeated in living memory. They have no qualms however about a more insidious 'peaceful' version

p)   Nato, the US and UK have ensured our safety, not the EU

q)   'right wing extremism' – please see London, Brussels, Paris, Instanbul, Syria for a definition of extremism

r)   Death toll post Brexit – 0 Death toll Europe post Brexit – 50, or whatever it is.

s)   Jo Cox. When it looked like we could win, a lone gunmen trashed our chances. If we were the US I'd call that suspicious. Yet no matter. She was played constantly all the time up to voting. Her birthday was voting day. You simply couldn't make it more emotional (bit like 9/11 is 911, US 999). People like symbolism. Except, have you heard one word from your 95% friends about Jo Cox, how Jo Cox would have wanted to run the referendum again, how so sad it is that Jo Cox died for nothing, how Jo Cox etc? No, she disappeared from the media and from Remain's string pulling the moment voting ended. RIP Jo Cox, finally.

t)   Cameron was essentially bounced into offering a referendum courtesy of Farage, who deserves a knighthood for services to democracy, regardless of our opinion of him.

u)   Remain by contrast raised no objection to the referendum beforehand. It was their referendum. They raised no objection to the bar (50%) or the margin (1 single vote if that's what it came down to, though even I would admit that was 'close'). Nor did they specify other 'special rules' to make it count. Only after they lost did they suddenly stand up and give all their reasons why it didn't count. Simple answer: we reserve the right to run any general election again and again until we get the 'right' result. We won, you lost, it's democracy.

v)   Seeking to overturn or ignore the result reveals the shamocracy, that we are a democratically elected autorcracy

w)   The margin was in fact a very solid result. Even with London, Home Counties, Scotland, Gibraltar, Northern Ireland voting Remain, it was 52:48, with a 72% turnout, and 36% of eligible votes 'won' (ie: 72% x 52%). You will see nonsense about how 'only' 36% voted to leave so it's not a majority, not a democracy. Nuff said: the principle of a vote in the western world in government is: the one with the most votes wins. People are trying to use eg: Congressional veto logic 'only overruled by 66%'. Fine, you want to go to the US or do it differently, that's for next time. These were the rules, we won, any objection is anti-democratic.

x)   They are allowed to be upset. After all they lost. As did England in the football. No reruns there, sorry.

y)   Comparison with elections: Cameron 2015: 66% turnout, 36% winning vote, 24% of people; Bush 2000: 50% turnout, MINUS 0.5% popular vote, 0.9% electoral vote, 24% of people. Referendum: 72% 4% 36: it was solid.

z)   The referendum to say no to a bunch of eurocrats telling us what to do was far more solid that the vote that gave the button and the world's most powerful military to Bush. And what he did with it? 9/11, Iraq, fourteen years of War on Terror, back to Instanbul last night.

Bottom line: We said 'we want a divorce'. We didn't say we intended to kill all first born of those not born of the beloved religion of John Cleese. We can still trade with Europeans, have sex with Europeans (both in the divorce metaphor and literally), have a great life basically. It's just that when Juncker summons 'all European nations' to issue his directive that 'we today signify our unity be an oath of allegiance of all military personnel to the EU', then we can simply look on and say how fascinating, and I wonder why the European peoples are putting up with it.

When Juncker issues a directive that only bananas from approved EU friendly nations are allowed to be imported, we can look on and take bananas from whoever we like.

When Junker issues a directive that ... you get the idea.

You might ask them: haven't you ever had a relationship when you were glad to be finally out?

That's how I feel. Results night was one of the most exciting and amazing of my life. I waited decades, literally, for such a night and never expected to see it.

Oh yes, last couple of things:

Like Agincourt, we secured a victory that according to the authorities we shouldn't have won.

We had the following against us:

The great and the good of both parties

Cameron, Corbyn

Former prime ministers Blair, Brown, Major

EU leaders Merkel, Juncker, Hollande

Brexit: Why We Won

The US President Obama

Sir Richard Branson, Sir Bob Geldof

JK Rowling, and the liberals

The Bank of England

The government statisticians and bureaucrats

The World Bank etc or whoever

American Corporate money (about which I'm pissed off... interfering in sovereign issues)

Everyone but everyone with weight and standing was clear that we should remain 'for the greater good'

Including Jo Cox.

We still were looking good, until Jo Cox. I never believed we'd survive that.

But we did.

So all I can say is, with everything that Remain had going for it, and it did have 'everything', all the power players in the entire world on its side...

... we still voted for freedom, the same freedom Obama enjoys, America enjoys, that it won from a foreign unelected power.

Yet we were supposed to cave.

We didn't. It was the greatest victory for democracy and common sense in our history.

And now everyone's determined to give it up out of fear for their wallets, fear that they won't be allowed to go skiing in Courchevel, fear that... it's endless, and it's nonsense.

The young are upset? Experience counts. Be glad your dad saved you.

Old white thickos won? Then England is lucky that it had such stout hearted warriors for democracy, for the effete had sold out, and are still determined to sell us out.

And as for London going independent... Scotland can do as it wishes, but Londinium, founded by the Romans, quickly became the seat of power for this nation. We have bled and died for that town, that city, that City, for millennia, and it has not been threatened by invasion since 1066.

That is our nation's capital, and the current occupants are temporary leaseholders. The land is ours. Destroy the buildings, but we may then have to stop you, leave by all means, but that land is ours by blood right: we died for it, and we died protecting Europe as we were led by its will.

Europe and Remain might care to remember that.

And of course I forgot a couple of key things:

If we were wrong and the politicians were right, why are they in turmoil, with Corbyn still in despite massive resignations and a 172:40 confidence vote against, with Cameron doing the decent thing in resigning and candidates using our will to secure the trophy that's being trampled by them into the mud in their haste to secure the top slot.

We didn't do it against them, but against their will: we voted out, implement article 50 now.

Recall why we raise two fingers, an ancient symbol of defiance from Agincourt.

The arrogant French boasted that they would cut the two fingers that pulled the bowstring of the hated archers, so deadly that each arrow had the force of a .303 rifle bullet, puncturing armour with ease.

After the victory against appalling odds, the archers raised their fingers to show they were still intact.

Against similarly appalling, if non-lethal, odds the ordinary British people raised two fingers to the elite, the liberals, the wallet-heads, and told them to go forth.

We did something they will never understand it seems: we said that no matter the cost, and it need not be high, we stood for something that is precious to Britain, to all humans, the right to freedom and self-determination.

Better yet, it may turn out to be an economic, as well as cultural, godsend.

Conclusion

We 'happy few' of seventeen million have every right to feel proud of what we achieved. Seventeen million, by the way, is fifty percent more people than voted for Cameron, giving him an outright majority.

It was a solid result, for sound reasons, and even Remainer analysts are having to change their tune.

The acrimony fom Remain immediately after the vote, and their continuing determination to undo the result, simply reveals how far from the fundamentals of freedom our more self-centred kin have strayed.

Andrew Mather

Feedback

Feel free to contact me at:
and.romeda@btconnect.com

Also by Andrew Mather

The following are other titles by Andrew Mather.

Brexit: Victory and Hope

The Leave Vote and Securing a Future

What is it going to take to turn an extraordinary result into an extraordinary or at least decent future? The answer lies not in the immediate actions of politicians but in the character of the Britons who had the courage to vote for Leave against all the authorities telling them to do otherwise.

In this book we look at a different perspective than that of the economists who tell us we risk dire results by our vote, and even from the core ideas that we covered in 'Brexit: Why We Won'. There is a divide in Britain, as there is in the world at large, but it is not the divide between left and right which is significant here, but that between controllers, those who love authority, and the ordinary independent people who do their best to get on with their lives with minimal outside interference.

Brexit: A Sound Decision

Nine Weeks On And Looking Good

The sky hasn't fallen, experts are having to revise their prognostications, countries are queuing up to manage trade negotiations with Britain, and May, a Remainer, nevertheless seems determined to honour the vote.

Emotions have subsided somewhat, though Remain still threaten to derail the result with an MP rebellion, or legal challenge. Sturgeon continues to do everything possible to cause strife and consternation.

It is by no means assured that we will get the clear break that Leave voters would like to see. It may indeed take years to unravel our ties with the EU, and to rework them into something more suitable to a sovereign nation dealing with a politicial superstate.

The issues remain, and we revisit them to provide a perhaps tidier, better organised summary than in the original Brexit: Why We Won, which was written in a hurry for good reason. Remain were up in arms.

Many still are, so it's still worth understanding the issues, and the sound reasons for our vote.

Experience Counts

Pedestrian Risk and Road Safety Policy

Not by coincidence there is a striking similarity between the themes of Brexit and those of Road Safety, whereby a majority of sensible, ordinary everyday drivers making informed decisions as to speed are told by those in authority that they're wrong, they're the danger, they should be doing what they're told and obeying the limits.

Yet the government's own figures give the lie to the mantra, and show that the government, controllers, those who love authority and having their say, are targeting the only key measure that can indeed be easily measured. They're targeting speeding drivers not because they're a material risk, but because they're the only ones they can easily target and prosecute.

Find out who the dangerous and lethal road users really are. It's not just Brexit where the government are more than happy to turn a blind eye to the facts for the sake of convenience and dogma.

Also on Facebook as Experience Counts.

Andrew Mather

Apostle of Camelot

Essene Camelot Series of Novels

A source once described a tale so fascinating that I decided to turn it into a novel. There was a brief window before this island became subject to Rome, where refugees from persecution in their homeland could take root in a quiet corner away from the Empire.

They shaped the future of this nation, and their legacy is the sense of fair play that Britons adhere to. Yet by fate or coincidence their nemesis, the arch persecutor of their kin, also ended up on these islands. By now he was a changed man, yet still in conflict with their ideals.

A tale more remarkable than the recognised Camelot myth and one based on events, some of which are recognised even by the Catholic church, this is not so much fiction as fictionalised.

The Essene family of the Nazarene Jesus did flee to Alexandria, were indeed deliberately set on a craft without oars, sails, food or water to die, and yet they survived to settle in Gaul and what would become Britannia.

Also on Facebook as Essene Camelot

The Dawkins Delusion

Beyond Religion and Science

There seems to be a common theme in many human affairs, that of the adversarial position. You are Left or Right, Remain or Leave, Religious or Atheist, and a great deal of emotion is expended vilifying the opposition, as the Brexit vote has shown.

To those polarised by the issue of Religion vs Atheism, a simple, common sense, pragmatic experience that goes beyond the mundane, the physical, is anathema. It is not God, so it is hated by religious folk; and it is not Science, so it is hated by Atheist folk.

Well, a little like the 'thicko' argument against Leave, I'm not a thicko, retain my faculty for analysis, and yet have thirty years background in a natural, useful phenomenon, that of acknowledging that we are more than just a body.

One source, that of the Essene Camelot series, has also provided a very elegant model that ties in the experience of the New Age, the leading edge ideas of Science (a ten-dimensional reality) and shows how they are all part of a simple, elegant framework.

911 Pentagon Strike

Fabricated evidence in US vs Moussaoui

It will gladden the hearts of Remainers to find one more excuse to deride and dismiss the author, but one thing I hate is deception, and one thing that fascinates me is the way in which societies are shaped.

Thus we see a common theme between Brexit, Road Safety, and 9/11 (the slash omitted deliberately in the title): they are all about authority, and the public being told a story, and the conflict between those who believe the official story, and those who investigate, do their own research, and apply their own common sense.

In each of those fields, those countering the official view are derided, yet at the end of the day, uncomfortable as it may be for those whose only weapon is derision, we have the facts on our side.

More than that, in this short book, I show the simplest proof of a criminal act by the US Department of Defense: it edited the security cameras shots and then submitted them in a criminal trial, a criminal offence.

Nuff said.

About The Author

Andrew Mather spent six years in finance, followed by many years as a consultant in finance and technology before committing a decade to inventing and proving an information technology designed to absorb information, integrating it into a single coherent source, a global brain.

As hobbies, his passion has been for flying and adventure that has taken him around the world, most memorably to Russia in the era of Glasnost to fly their jets, to the USA to fly the Mustang, and courtesy of a wonderful gift from his brother, a flight in the Grace Spitfire.

His other adventure has been to be nudged into a realm that challenged his mathematical and analytical background, and yet has been a companion now for some thirty years.

As science delves more accurately into the nature of reality, it is probing ever more deeply into a mystery, rarely if ever acknowledging that it is alive and not inert.

Andrew's pleasure has been to meet with and listen to a number of sources whose wisdom, humour and integrity have greatly enriched his life.

15522887R00058

Printed in Poland
by Amazon Fulfillment
Poland Sp. z o.o., Wrocław